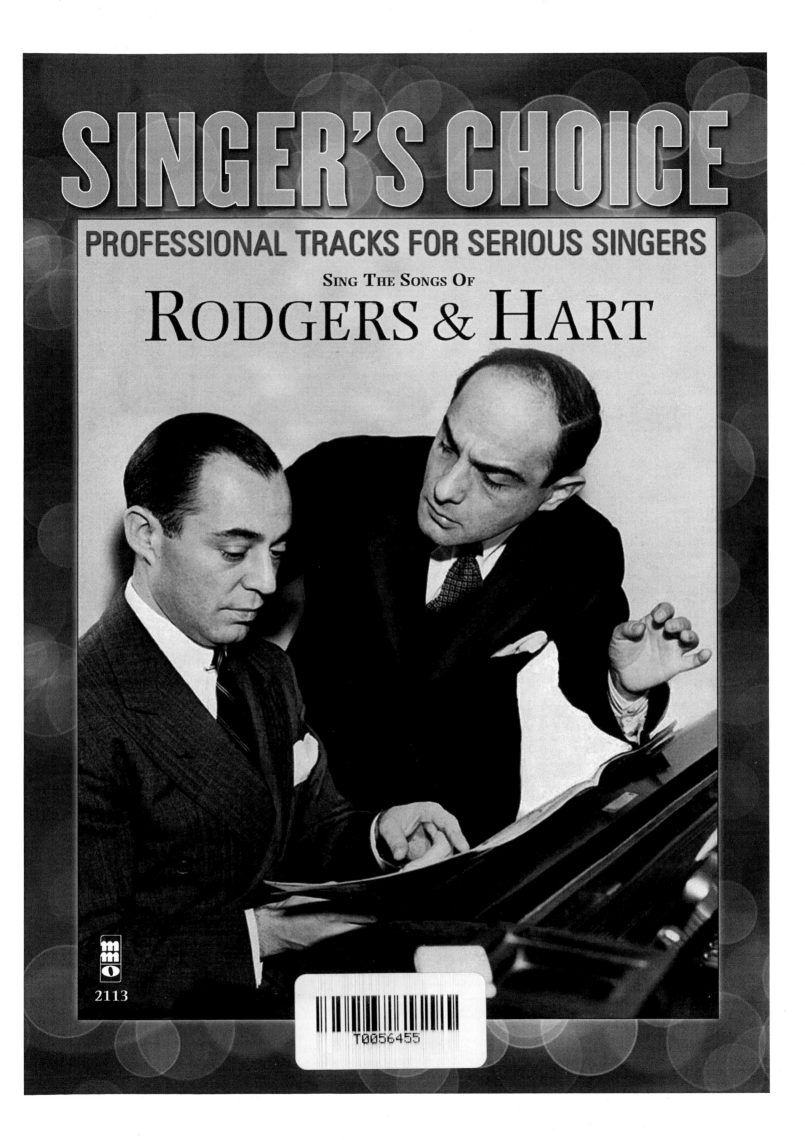

SINGER'S CHOICE

PROFESSIONAL TRACKS FOR SERIOUS SINGERS

SING THE SONGS OF
RODGERS & HART

2113

- notes continued from back cover

In 1925 Rodgers & Hart wrote for the Garrick Gaieties, a fundraising revue that included their first hit, "Manhattan." The 1926 version of the Garrick Gaieties included "Mountain Greenery." For the next five years the team of Rodgers & Hart wrote for several major shows including Dearest Enemy, The Girl Friend, Peggy-Ann, A Connecticut Yankee and Present Arms. Among their songs from that era were "Blue Room," "My Heart Stood Still," "Thou Swell," "A Ship Without A Sail," "Dancing On The Ceiling" and 'You Took Advantage Of Me."

Seeing greater work opportunities in Hollywood, Rodgers & Hart began writing for the movies in the early 1930s. While few today would remember the movies Love Me Tonight, The Phantom President and Hallelujah, I'm A Bum (which starred Al Jolson), the songs "Lover" and "Isn't It Romantic" became standards. One of their biggest hits, "Blue Moon," was their only significant song not introduced on Broadway or in movies.

The team returned triumphantly to Broadway in 1935 where they had one hit after another including the shows Jumbo, On Your Toes, I Married An Angel, The Boys From Syracuse, and Pal Joey. This period yielded such classics as "My Romance," "There's A Small Hotel," "Little Girl Blue," "Where Or When," "My Funny Valentine," "The Lady Is A Tramp," "Have You Met Miss Jones," "Spring Is Here," "Falling In Love With Love," "This Can't Be Love," "I Didn't Know What Time It Was," "It Never Entered My Mind," "I Could Write A Book," and "Bewitched, Bothered and Bewildered." It was quite a string of superior songs, all of which are still performed today. The material ranged from love songs to the ironic "The Lady Is A Tramp," the wistful "Falling In Love With Love," the humorous "This Can't Be Love" and the rather sad "It Never Entered My Mind."

In 1940 Rodgers was still just 38 while Hart was 45. With luck their successes should have continued for another 20 or 30 years. But Hart's declining health and erratic behavior was making it impossible for Rodgers. They collaborated for the last time for 1942's By Jupiter which included "Nobody's Heart Belongs To Me." However when Hart turned down the opportunity to turn the story Green Grow The Lilacs into a musical, Rodgers had enough. For the first time in his life, he chose to collaborate with a different lyricist than Hart. He teamed up with Oscar Hammerstein III. for the play, which was renamed Oklahoma.

Lorenz Hart died in 1943 when he was just 48, shortly after Oklahoma became a giant success. Rodgers and Hammerstein would build their own rather impressive musical legacy which lasted until Hammerstein's passing in 1960.

– Scott Yanow,
author of 11 books including Swing,
Jazz On Film and Jazz On Record 1917-76

Sing The Songs Of
Rodgers & Hart

CONTENTS

ISBN 978-1-941566-10-7

MMO 2113

I Didn't Know What Time It Was

Words and Music by
Lorenz Hart and Richard Rodgers

MMO 2113

My Funny Valentine

Words and Music by
Lorenz Hart and Richard Rodgers

6

Nobody's Heart Belongs To Me

Words and Music by
Lorenz Hart and Richard Rodgers

A Ship Without A Sail

Words and Music by
Lorenz Hart and Richard Rodgers

8

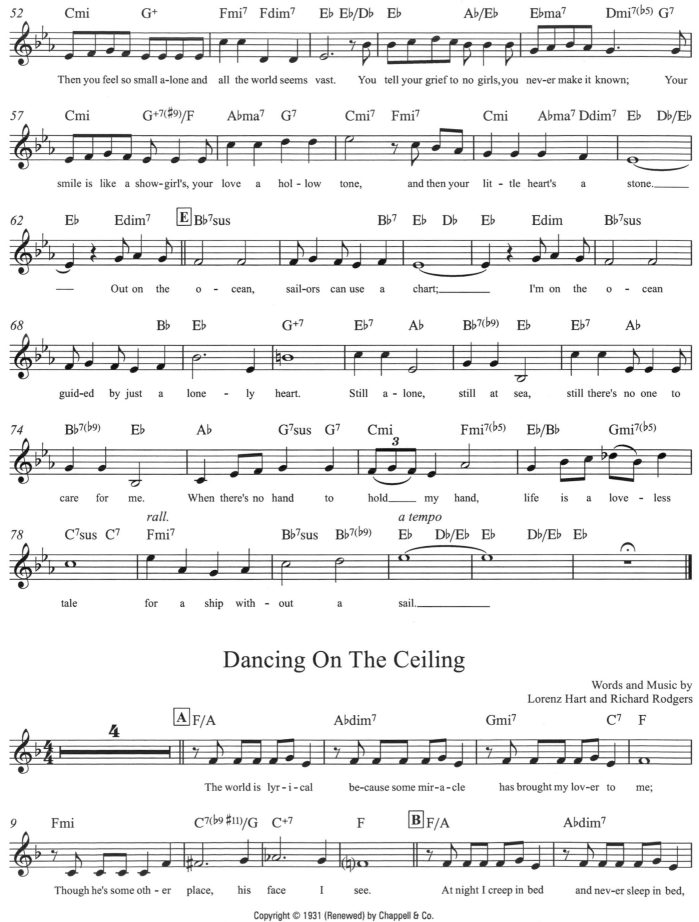

Dancing On The Ceiling

Words and Music by
Lorenz Hart and Richard Rodgers

Then you feel so small a-lone and all the world seems vast. You tell your grief to no girls, you nev-er make it known; Your

smile is like a show-girl's, your love a hol-low tone, and then your lit-tle heart's a stone.

— Out on the o-cean, sail-ors can use a chart; I'm on the o-cean

guid-ed by just a lone-ly heart. Still a-lone, still at sea, still there's no one to

care for me. When there's no hand to hold my hand, life is a love-less

tale for a ship with-out a sail.

The world is lyr-i-cal be-cause some mir-a-cle has brought my lov-er to me;

Though he's some oth-er place, his face I see. At night I creep in bed and nev-er sleep in bed,

It Never Entered My Mind

Words and Music by
Lorenz Hart and Richard Rodgers

There's A Small Hotel

Words and Music by
Lorenz Hart and Richard Rodgers

12

Where Or When

Words and Music by
Lorenz Hart and Richard Rodgers

13

MMO 2113

Other Great Songs from this MMO Series

Vol. 1 - Sing the Songs of George & Ira Gershwin .... MMO 2101
Somebody Loves Me • The Man I Love • Bidin' My Time • Someone To Watch Over Me • I've Got A Crush On You • But Not For Me • S'Wonderful • Fascinatin' Rhythm

Vol. 2 - Sing the Songs of Cole Porter .... MMO 2102
Night And Day • You Do Something To Me • Just One Of Those Things • Begin The Beguine • What Is This Thing Called Love • Let's Do It • Love For Sale • I Get A Kick Out Of You

Vol. 3 - Sing the Songs of Irving Berlin .... MMO 2103
Cheek To Cheek • Steppin' Out With My Baby • Let's Face The Music And Dance • Change Partners • Let Yourself Go • Say It Isn't So • Isn't This A Lovely Day • This Year's Kisses • Be Careful, It's My Heart

Vol. 4 - Sing the Songs of Harold Arlen .... MMO 2104
I've Got The World On A String • Down With Love • As Long As I Live • Stormy Weather • I've Got A Right To Sing The Blues • The Blues In The Night • Out Of This World • Come Rain Or Come Shine • My Shining Hour • Hooray For Love

Vol. 5 - Sing More Songs by George & Ira Gershwin, Vol. 2 .... MMO 2105
Of Thee I Sing • Embraceable You • Oh, Lady Be Good • How Long Has This Been Going On? • Summertime • Love Walked In • Nice Work If You Can Get It • I Got Rhythm

Vol. 6 - Sing the Songs of Duke Ellington .... MMO 2106
Do Nothin' Until You Hear From Me • I Got It Bad (And That Ain't Good) • I Let A Song Go Out Of My Heart • It Don't Mean A Thing (If It Ain't Got That Swing) • Mood Indigo • Solitude • Sophisticated Lady • Don't Get Around Much Anymore

Vol. 7 - Sing the Songs of Fats Waller .... MMO 2107
I'm Gonna Sit Right Down And Write Myself A Letter • I've Got A Feeling I'm Falling • Squeeze Me • S'posin' • Two Sleepy People • Ain't Misbehavin' (I'm Savin' My Love For You) • Honeysuckle Rose • I Can't Give You Anything But Love • It's A Sin To Tell A Lie

Vol. 8 - Sing the Songs of Cole Porter, Vol. 2 .... MMO 2108
You're The Top • Easy To Love • Friendship • Anything Goes • Blow, Gabriel, Blow • You're The Top (Jazz Version) • I Get A Kick Out Of You • Anything Goes (Jazz Version)

Vol. 9 - Sing the Songs of Jimmy McHugh .... MMO 2109
It's A Most Unusual Day • You're a Sweetheart • Don't Blame Me • I Feel A Song Coming On • I'm in the Mood for Love • I Can't Give You Anything But Love • I Can't Believe That You're in Love with Me • On the Sunny Side of the Street • I Must Have That Man

Vol. 10 - Sing the Songs of Jerome Kern .... MMO 2110
A Fine Romance • Smoke Gets In Your Eyes • The Last Time I Saw Paris • The Way You Look Tonight • Yesterdays • The Folks Who Live On The Hill • Make Believe • I'm Old Fashioned • All The Things You Are • They Didn't Believe Me

Vol. 11 - Sing the Songs of Johnny Mercer .... MMO 2111
Come Rain or Come Shine • Charade • The Days of Wine and Roses • Dream • I'm Old Fashioned • I Wanna Be Around • Jeepers Creepers • Moon River • One For My Baby

Vol. 12 - Sing the Songs of Johnny Mercer, Vol. 2 .... MMO 2112
The Autumn Leaves • Fools Rush In • I Remember You • My Shining Hour • Skylark • Tangerine • Too Marvelous For Words • Mr. Meadowlark

Vol. 13 - Sing the Songs of Rodgers & Hart .... MMO 2113
I Didn't Know What Time It Was • My Funny Valentine • Nobody's Heart Belongs To Me • A Ship Without A Sail • Dancing On The Ceiling • It Never Entered My Mind • There's A Small Hotel • Where Or When

Vol. 14 - Sing the Songs of Harry Warren .... MMO 2114
You'll Never Know • The More I See You • I Wish I Knew • This Is Always • I Had The Craziest Dream • I Only Have Eyes For You • Jeepers Creepers • That's Amore • Serenade In Blue

Music Minus One
50 Executive Boulevard · Elmsford, New York 10523-1325
914-592-1188 · e-mail: info@musicminusone.com
www.musicminusone.com

MMO 2113

ISBN 978-1-941566-10-7